A BLUE BANNER
BIOGRAPHY

50 Cent

Mary Boone

P.O. Box 196
Hockessin, Delaware 19707
Visit us on the web: www.mitchelllane.com
Comments? email us: mitchelllane@mitchelllane.com

Mitchell Lane PUBLISHERS

Printing   3   4   5   6   7   8   9

Blue Banner Biographies

Alan Jackson	Alicia Keys	Allen Iverson
Ashanti	Ashlee Simpson	Ashton Kutcher
Avril Lavigne	Bernie Mac	Beyoncé
Bow Wow	Britney Spears	Carrie Underwood
Chris Brown	Christina Aguilera	Christopher Paul Curtis
Ciara	Clay Aiken	Condoleezza Rice
Daniel Radcliffe	David Ortiz	Derek Jeter
Eminem	Eve	Fergie (Stacy Ferguson)
50 Cent	Gwen Stefani	Ice Cube
Jamie Foxx	Ja Rule	Jay-Z
Jennifer Lopez	Jessica Simpson	J. K. Rowling
Jodie Foster	Johnny Depp	JoJo
Justin Berfield	Justin Timberlake	Kate Hudson
Keith Urban	Kelly Clarkson	Kenny Chesney
Lance Armstrong	Lindsay Lohan	Mariah Carey
Mario	Mary J. Blige	Mary-Kate and Ashley Olsen
Michael Jackson	Miguel Tejada	Missy Elliott
Nancy Pelosi	Nelly	Orlando Bloom
P. Diddy	Paris Hilton	Peyton Manning
Queen Latifah	Ron Howard	Rudy Giuliani
Sally Field	Selena	Shakira
Shirley Temple	Tim McGraw	Usher
Zach Efron		

Library of Congress Cataloging-in-Publication Data
Boone, Mary.
    50 Cent/ by Mary Boone.
        p. cm. — (Blue banner biography)
    Includes bibliographical references (p.) and index.
    ISBN 1-58415-523-X (library bound: alk. paper)
    1. 50 Cent (Musician)—Juvenile literature. 2. Rap musicians—United States—Biography—
Juvenile literature. I. Title. II. Series.
ML3930.A13B66 2007
782. 421649092—dc22
[B]   2006014800

ISBN-13: 9781584155232

ABOUT THE AUTHOR: Mary Boone has written eight books for young adults, including biographies about Hilary Duff, Lindsay Lohan, and Raven. She also has written for magazines including *People, Teen People, Mary-Kate and Ashley*, and *Entertainment Weekly*. Boone lives in Tacoma, Washington. When she's not writing she enjoys running, swimming, and being outdoors with her husband, Mitch, and their two children, Eve and Eli.

PHOTO CREDITS: Cover: Gareth Davies/Getty Images; p. 4 Julie Jacobson/Associated Press; p. 7 Barry Talesnick/Globe Photos; p. 10 Tim Mosenfelder/Getty Images; p. 13 Fernando Leon/Getty Images; p. 15 Frank Micelotta/Getty Images; p. 17 Gareth Davies/Getty Images; p. 21 Peter Kramer/ Getty Images; p. 25 Jennifer Graylock/Associated Press

CONTENTS

In 2003, at the MTV Music Video Awards, 50 won Best New Artist and Best Rap Video of the Year for "In Da Club." He had come a long way from being a teenage drug hustler who seemed destined for a life in prison.

Terrible Odds

Almost as soon as he was released from prison on drug charges, Curtis Jackson was back on the streets dealing. He was still on parole and riding his Suzuki motorcycle down the strip in Jamaica, Queens, New York, when a squad car pulled up beside him with its lights on and its siren blasting.

"Pull ov—"

Curtis floored it before the words were out of the loudspeaker. He didn't know what the cops wanted, but he knew even the slightest violation would send him back to prison. The teenager ran stoplights, sped down sidewalks, and gunned it at more than 100 miles an hour. He ditched his bike in a friend's yard and sprinted to his house, where he hid in the attic and listened as a police officer told his grandfather that his grandson was a suspect in a homicide.

Curtis hadn't killed anybody, but as he hunched down in that attic, he realized he needed a new life and a new line of work. That's when he started to think about making money from entertainment.

Curtis James Jackson III became the controversial and world-famous rapper 50 Cent, but the road to fame was not without challenges.

Drugs and danger were central to Curtis's childhood. His mother, Sabrina, was just fifteen years old when he was born on July 6, 1975. When he was old enough to ask about his father, she was quick to tell him he didn't have one.

Sabrina Jackson was a big-time drug hustler who left young Curtis to live with her parents and the boy's eight aunts and uncles. She didn't come around often, except to bring gifts and cash to the son she called "Boo-Boo."

"She used to substitute finances for time," 50 told *Rolling Stone*. "Every time I seen her, it was some-thing new for me. Christmas every day. She put jewelry on me early."

When Curtis was eight, someone went home with Sabrina, slipped something in her drink that knocked her out, closed the windows, turned on the gas, and left her to die. Curtis is certain her death was drug-related.

The boy's grandparents tried to steer him away from life on the streets, but he'd grown accustomed to the clothes, bikes, and jewelry his mother bought him. When he was eleven, some older guys in the neighborhood gave him some cocaine to sell. He was still in school, so he could only hustle between three and six p.m., when his grandparents thought he was playing with friends.

"The more I did it, the easier it got," he writes in his autobiography *From Pieces to Weight*. "At first, I was able to do small things like buy snacks and fast food. Then I was able to get sneakers and clothes. Then I started getting little handheld video games, but that didn't make sense: I didn't have time to play any games; I was too busy selling coke."

Curtis was a sophomore at Andrew Jackson High School when he was first busted for possession of a

A far cry from the days when he sold drugs so that he could buy new clothes, 50 Cent was a celebrity guest at Child *magazine's 2006 fashion week show. He and his son, Marquise, modeled his G-Unit clothing line.*

controlled substance. He was suspended from school for two weeks — during which he sold more crack than his normal school-day schedule allowed — and was sentenced to eighteen months' probation. He was transferred to another school, but by that point it didn't matter. For Curtis, school had become a fashion show: He'd sell enough drugs to buy new clothes and then pop in for a day to show them off.

Curtis knew if he continued to sell drugs, he'd end up dead or in prison.

Curtis dropped out of school after the tenth grade and became an even bigger player on the street. When he was eighteen, he was making $5,000 a day selling crack and heroin. He bought himself cars and guns and became an impressive amateur boxer.

In 1994, he was arrested on drug charges twice in three weeks. Curtis was facing a three- to nine-year jail term when his attorney worked a deal that would cut his sentence if he participated in a military-style rehabilitation program. He made it through the program, earned his general equivalency diploma (GED), and was back on the street in six months. He wasn't exactly reformed, but Curtis knew if he continued to sell drugs, he'd end up dead or in prison.

"It was coming," he told *Rolling Stone.* "Long as you stay there, you don't beat the odds."

Hitting the Right Note

*C*urtis messed around with rhymes and beats for a few years, but when his girlfriend Tanisha got pregnant, he realized he had to stop thinking about making a career change and actually do something about it. Curtis had grown up around the drug game, and he didn't want to raise his child anywhere near that world.

Curtis knew what kind of music he liked. He was a fan of Snoop Doggy Dogg's *Doggystyle,* Notorious B.I.G.'s *Ready to Die,* and the political rhymes of KRS-ONE. But when it came to putting together a song, he didn't have a clue.

In 1996, Curtis had a chance meeting with Jam Master Jay, the founder and DJ of the influential hip-hop group Run-DMC. Jay liked Curtis and taught him how to build verses and count beats. He also signed the young musician to his production company.

Curtis James Jackson III became 50 Cent, a name he took from Kelvin Martin, a Brooklyn crook who used to rob rappers. He says the name is also a metaphor for change.

"I decided, I'm going to change the game," he writes in *From Pieces to Weight.* "That was how I felt. I knew that

Fiddy used his first songs to poke fun at other rappers. His style earned him a record deal and made him a target for those unhappy with his very public criticism.

no one was talking about the stuff I was talking about in the way that I was."

While other rappers were singing about getting rich and becoming famous, 50 Cent—also known as 50 or Fiddy—was rapping about life on the streets and players who were still very much part of that scene.

In 1999, a producing team called Track Masters heard 50 Cent and got him a deal at Columbia Records. He quickly began work on his debut album, *Power of the Dollar.* Three singles were released, and one, "How to Rob," earned a lot of attention. Its lyrics detailed how Fiddy would rob dozens of wealthy entertainers, including Brian McKnight, Will Smith, Bobby Brown, RZA, and Juvenile. The record established 50 Cent as a funny, fearless gangster. Still, some weren't laughing.

Fiddy soon found himself in feuds with rappers Ja Rule and Jay-Z and drug lord Kenneth "Supreme" McGriff. One night, while 50 was at the Manhattan recording studio Hit Factory 50, he got in a fight with Ja Rule's crew and was stabbed. The injury wasn't serious, and Fiddy found comfort in the fact that people were talking about him. His album was about to be released and he was on the brink of stardom—or so he thought. On May 24, 2000, everything changed.

> In 1999, a producing team called Track Masters heard 50 Cent and got him a deal at Columbia Records.

The rapper was in a friend's car in front of his grandparents' house when someone came up beside him with a gun cocked. The shooter hit him nine times at close range; 50 took bullets in the hand, hip, calf, and chest, plus one to the face that went though his cheek and into his mouth.

Columbia Records executives worried that, even if Fiddy survived, he'd be disabled or too disfigured to perform. The label dropped him and never released his album. He had no record deal and no money, so he went back to selling drugs to support himself. The setback might have soured most in the industry, but 50 was more determined than ever.

He spent nearly two weeks in the hospital and hobbled out with the help of a walker. After six months of physical therapy, he was able to walk on his own. He began doing push-ups, pull-ups and sit-ups, which helped chisel his now famous muscular physique. He also made daily visits to the gun range to keep his aim accurate.

"I was never going to be caught unawares again," he writes in *From Pieces to Weight*.

Fiddy's pal Sha Money XL had a studio on Long Island. Soon 50 was recording mix tapes. He started by giving away free samples on the streets of New York. He later sent tapes to about fifty DJs across the country.

> **The shooter hit him nine times at close range; 50 took bullets in the hand, hip, calf, and chest, plus one to the face.**

The G-Unit lends its celebrity status to a 2004 New York City clothing drive. Group members are longtime friends 50 Cent (left), Lloyd Banks, and Tony Yayo (right).

He formed a posse with lifelong friends Tony Yayo (Marvin Bernard) and Lloyd Banks (Christopher Lloyd) and named it the G-Unit after the animated band Gorillaz. The three created music that soon could be heard pounding from car stereos and open windows across the city. Their songs were being played on the radio, first during the mix shows and later as part of radio stations' nightly countdowns.

Fiddy knew mix tapes weren't supposed to get that sort of attention. He took it as a sign that his career was on the upswing. He was right.

The Eminem Connection

One of 50 Cent's mix tapes eventually made its way to rapper/producer Eminem, who had recently combined his Shady Records label with Dr. Dre's Aftermath label. Eminem quickly got onto New York's hip-hop radio circuit with the message that 50 Cent was his favorite rapper of the moment.

"It didn't take a genius to know that 50 was going to be big," Dre told *Newsweek*. "He had the style, the flow and the attitude—and he wanted it badly."

Thanks in large part to Eminem's praise, a twenty-six-year-old Fiddy found himself in the middle of a bidding war among a number of record labels. He ultimately signed a million-dollar contract with Eminem and Dre, two of the rappers he most respected and knew he could trust.

"When they signed me, they could have been purchasing a big problem," Fiddy writes in *From Pieces to Weight*. "I could've went in another direction, [messed] everything up, and made them look crazy. . . . A lot of my success is credited to Eminem, regardless of how people look at it or feel about it. He did make the situation happen."

Dre and Eminem coproduced 50's debut album, *Get Rich or Die Tryin'*, and each produced a few tracks for it.

Even before *Get Rich* hit stores, Em debuted Fiddy on the sound track for *8 Mile,* a movie in which Eminem stars with Brittany Murphy, Kim Basinger, and Mekhi Phifer. "Wanksta" had previously been included on a mix tape; when it was released as a single in 2002, it peaked at

In 2004, 50 Cent, left, joined pals Eminem, center, and Dr. Dre at the New York City launch of Shade 45, a new satellite radio station. Dre and Eminem signed Fiddy to his first big record contract and coproduced his debut album, Get Rich or Die Tryin'.

number 13 on Billboard's Hot 100 and became 50 Cent's first Top 20 single.

Following "Wanksta," Fiddy released "In Da Club" from *Get Rich.* The song soared to number 1 on the Billboard charts, and within a week of its release broke a Billboard magazine record as the "most listened-to song in radio history." Already 50 was touring the world, watching his music break the language barrier in places like Japan and Germany. The enormous success of "In Da Club" forced Dre and Eminem to move up *Get Rich*'s release date to prevent bootlegging. But the success of his first two singles was just the beginning.

> **In its first week, Get Rich or Die Tryin' sold 872,000 copies as stores struggled to keep up with the demand.**

In its first week, *Get Rich or Die Tryin'* sold 872,000 copies as stores struggled to keep up with the demand. It broke the record for first-week sales of any major label debut in the history of Nielsen SoundScan, an information system that tracks music sales and provides data for the Billboard charts. *Get Rich* was certified platinum (1 million copies sold) in its second week. It has since sold more than 11 million copies.

"I remember thinking that I knew I was going to sell 5 million copies and I said that on the promotional DVD," he told *Newsweek.* "But then I tried to clean it up by saying,

He thought he was destined for big things, but even 50 Cent couldn't predict how big. His album Get Rich or Die Tryin' *was the second best selling album across all genres in 2005.*

'If not this album, some other album would see 5 million.' Cause I was like, 'Don't play yourself and look stupid.' Eleven million wasn't even in my mind frame."

Following on the heels of *Get Rich*'s success, 50 worked in partnership with Dre and Eminem to form G-Unit Records and released an album with Lloyd Banks, Tony Yayo, and Young Buck (David Darnell Brown). It sold 2 million copies.

When it came time to release 50's *The Massacre* in 2005, fans were hungry. In fact, when bootleg copies began appearing in major markets, its release was bumped up five days.

"Fans want instant gratification, especially when they are fiending for my music. They'll even risk buying the wrong [stuff] from bootleggers," 50 Cent said in a statement from his record label. "I want them to have the real thing as soon as possible."

Get Rich or Die Tryin' ultimately became the second best selling album of 2005 with 4.8 million copies sold.

The album featured guest appearances by 50's G-Unit crew, protégé The Game (Jayceon Taylor), Olivia (Olivia Longott), and Jamie Foxx. It ultimately became the second best selling album of 2005 with 4.8 million copies sold.

And, of course, Eminem was there for 50 as coproducer, friend, and role model.

"I kind of look to Eminem to gauge how I should respond to success," the twenty-nine-year-old rapper said at a press conference while on tour in Asia. "He's had even bigger success than I have in some areas. He's been extremely helpful to me to kind of stay levelheaded."

Controversy
Wherever He Goes

*A*mid all his chart-topping success, 50 Cent continued to make headlines outside the music studio and stage. The media was fascinated by his life story. Major articles about him ran in mainstream publications, including the *New York Times* and *Newsweek*. He became a frequent guest on daytime talk shows, and his videos were in heavy rotation on MTV.

Still, controversy surrounded the man from Jamaica, Queens.

Fiddy clashed with dozens of artists. He used his music to poke fun at celebrities including Ja Rule, Spike Lee, R. Kelly, The Game, Lil' Kim, Cadillac Tah, Black Child, Fat Joe, Nas, and Jadakiss.

He was linked to Jam Master Jay's October 2002 murder and was jailed on New Year's Eve 2002 for gun possession. The FBI interrogated him while they were investigating the relationship between Murder, Inc., and former drug dealer Kenneth "Supreme" McGriff.

His music was labeled "too violent" when a twenty-four-year-old man was shot dead after seeing 50's 2003 Toronto concert. He pleaded no contest to assault charges in 2004 and was ordered to take anger management classes.

A man was shot and killed in the lobby of a Pittsburgh-area theater showing 50's *Get Rich or Die Tryin'* movie. Billboards for the film were taken down in a handful of cities after complaints that they promoted gun violence and gang activity.

> *A member of Canada's Federal House of Commons tried to stop Fiddy's 2005 Canadian tour.*

A member of Canada's Federal House of Commons tried to stop Fiddy's 2005 Canadian tour by denying the singer access to the country. The politician failed, but the G-Unit wasn't so lucky. More than half the crew was held up at the border.

In 2006 Fiddy got slapped with a lawsuit claiming parts of "In Da Club," from the album *Get Rich or Die Tryin'*, were stolen from a song written by 2 Live Crew founder Luther Campbell.

He started wearing a bulletproof vest, as did his son, Marquise. He spent $100,000 apiece to have his two cars bulletproofed.

The list goes on.

Fiddy insists controversy is just part of the game when you're one of the world's wealthiest, most popular rappers.

"Hip-hop is competitive so they are watching whoever falls into the spot," he told *Murder Dog* magazine. "Rappers condition themselves like fighters. All of them feel like they are the best. This is just hip-hop. When you fall into a position where you might be considered the champ at the moment they start to target at you. That is what I have been dealing with. Behind the scenes people will say things and do things out of place. I feel like if I don't address it then I'm encouraging them to be even more

Fiddy has found himself at the center of considerable controversy, including feuds with a number of fellow rappers. In 2005, 50 Cent, left, and The Game, right, set aside their differences and spoke publicly about the need for peace. As a sign of their sincerity, the two presented checks to Dr. Walter Turnbull, founder of the Boys Choir of Harlem, in support of that organization.

disrespectful. . . . Some people develop a king complex. They are feeling that they are so big that they shouldn't say anything back. I'm still competitive."

Fiddy did let his competitive guard down for a moment in October 2005, when he and The Game publicly ended a feud that had escalated to gunfire. The two rappers, appearing at Harlem's Schomburg Center for Research in Black Culture, apologized to each other, spoke about the need for peace, and shook hands.

Elliott Wilson, editor of the hip-hop magazine *XXL*, told the *Associated Press* the public apology was significant because "it is the first time we've seen 50 publicly take a step back."

The Game–50 Cent peace summit came at the same time Fiddy announced the creation of the G-Unity Foundation, Inc., an organization designed to invest in inner-city nonprofits that help people overcome obstacles and improve their lives.

"I realized that if I'm going to be effective at that, I have to overcome some of my own [obstacles]," 50 said in a statement released by his record label. "Game and I need to set an example in the community."

> *Fiddy announced the creation of the G-Unity Foundation, Inc., an organization designed to invest in inner-city nonprofits.*

Beyond the Music

*F*iddy boasts that he's never filled out a job application—never needed to. But if he did, what a resume he'd have: drug dealer, boxer, rapper, record mogul, video game developer, clothing designer, movie star, author, and more.

He may not have liked school, but when it comes to business, he does his homework. His empire now includes G-Unit Clothing Co., a shoe deal with Reebok, the semi-autobiographical movie *Get Rich or Die Tryin'*, video games, a best-selling ring tone, Formula 50 vitamin water, and albums recorded by G-Unit members.

When he signed his contract with Shady/Aftermath, the first thing he did was spend $110,000 for a worldwide trademark for G-Unit. It's an investment that seems to be paying off. His clothing line, for example, earned him more than $50 million in sales in its first year of operation. His athletic shoes brought in around $20 million in sales in 2004 alone.

"The media portrays him to be this monster but he's nothing like that," Olivia told *YRB* magazine. She teamed up with 50 on the single "Candy Shop." "He's a sweetheart. Once you get to know him you think he went to Harvard. He's got so many good deals."

His newest deals include another autobiography and a partnership with MTV/Pocket Books to create G-Unit Books, an imprint that publishes novellas and graphic novels focusing on street life.

"Fiction is the next natural extension for [50 Cent]," Pocket Books publisher Louise Burke told *New York Business.* "His audience has bought everything he's ever produced."

Interscope Records President Jimmy Iovine calls 50 one of the best businessmen he's ever worked with. "He's got a game plan for whatever happens," Iovine told *Newsweek.*

Interscope Records President Jimmy Iovine calls 50 one of the best businessmen he's ever worked with.

Even when things don't seem to be going his way— like when his *Get Rich* movie billboards were criticized for glorifying violence—Fiddy seems to come out on top. When Paramount Pictures gave in to protesters and took down some of the billboards, 50 told Reuters News Service: "I do appreciate it. They are talking about it on media outlets that I didn't have plans to market the movie to. They are helping me out."

With his many tattoos and gold chains, Fiddy's onstage persona always seems ready to party. Businessman Fiddy, however, doesn't smoke, drink, or do drugs. He's savvy enough to know packaging plays a huge role in marketing, so he eats right, takes multivitamins, and pumps iron to maintain his muscular build.

After growing up with next to nothing, Fiddy is now worth more than $60 million. He used some of that cash

As Fiddy's popularity has grown, so have his business holdings. In addition to a record label, he now has a clothing company, book imprint, video games, and more. In 2005, he attended this event at New York City's Virgin Megastore, where he signed copies of his autobiography, From Pieces to Weight: Once Upon a Time in Southside Queens.

to buy a twenty-one-bedroom Farmington, Connecticut, mansion from boxer Mike Tyson. He moved his grandparents to a new house and bought them both new cars.

"But you can't repay them in finances," he told *Blender* magazine. "I love them dearly. Maybe I'll repay them when they become so old that they can't take care of themselves—then I'll take care of them."

Fiddy remembers a time, not so long ago, when he hid out in his basement bedroom, tapping out beats and writing rhymes in his head.

> *"There's a point at which only I believed in me, but I envisioned things and worked until they started to materialize."*

"My grandparents looked at me as a dreamer, like, 'He's over there buggin','" he told *King* magazine. "There's a point at which only I believed in me, but I envisioned things and worked until they started to materialize."

These days, the drug-dealer-turned-musician is surrounded by believers eager to hear his next album, watch his next movie, or buy his next fashion product. His fans—and even those rappers with whom he frequently battles—know they haven't heard the last of Sabrina Jackson's only son.

"This is just the beginning," Fiddy told *Sync* magazine. "I can do a lot more, man. I haven't even used my full marketing skills yet."

CHRONOLOGY

1975 Curtis James Jackson III is born July 6 in Queens, New York

1984 Mother, Sabrina, a drug dealer, is murdered

1988 Curtis begins dealing drugs and is arrested for it

1994 Is arrested on felony drug charges twice in three weeks; decides to get away from drugs and try hip-hop

1996 Meets Jam Master Jay, who signs him to his JMJ Records label

1997 His son Marquise is born

1999 Begins work on his debut album *Power of the Dollar*; three singles are released, and one, "How to Rob," attracts attention for its lyrics naming other rappers

2000 Is stabbed at the Hit Factory Studio and soon after is shot nine times; Columbia decides not to release *Power of the Dollar* and cuts ties with the entertainer; he forms the G-Unit and begins releasing underground recordings

2002 Signs a contract worth more than $1 million with Eminem and Dr. Dre's Shady/Aftermath label (which is part of Interscope); is a suspect in Jam Master Jay's murder

2003 *Get Rich or Die Tryin'* is released; a record-breaking 872,000 albums sells in the first five days; G-Unit Records becomes another label for Interscope

2004 Launches Formula 50 vitamin water

2005 *The Massacre* is the second best selling album of the year; four 50 Cent songs rank among radio's year-end Top 20

2005 Releases *Get Rich or Die Tryin'* movie and sound track; releases a memoir about his life called *From Pieces to Weight: Once Upon a Time in Southside Queens*; creates G-Unity Foundation to benefit inner-city nonprofits

2006 Teams up with Glaceau (the company that sells Formula 50) to encourage good nutrition by offering a $100,000 scholarship to the student chef who creates the best healthy school lunch recipe

DISCOGRAPHY

Albums
2000 *Power of the Dollar* (unreleased)
2002 *Guess Who's Back* (mix tape)
50 Cent Is the Future (mix tape)
No Mercy, No Fear (mix tape)
2003 *50 Cent: The New Breed* (3-track CD)
Get Rich or Die Tryin'
2005 *The Massacre*

Sound Track Contributions
2002 *8 Mile*
"Love Me" (with Obie Trice and Eminem)
"Places to Go"
"Wanksta"
2003 *Cradle 2 The Grave*
"Follow Me Gangster"
2004 *Barbershop 2: Back in Business*
"Unconditionally" (as G-Unit)

FILMOGRAPHY

Movies
2005 *Get Rich or Die Tryin'*
The Game: Documentary
2006 *Home of the Brave*

Video Game
2005 *50 Cent: Bulletproof* (voice)

AWARDS

2003 American Music Awards for Favorite Rap/Hip-Hop Album and Favorite Male Rap/Hip-Hop Artist

MTV Video Music Awards for Best Rap Video and Best New Artist

World Music Awards for Best Artist, Best Pop Male Artist, Best R&B Artist, Best Rap/Hip-Hop Artist and Best New Artist

BET Awards for Best New Artist and Best Male Hip-Hop Artist

Vibe Awards for Artist of the Year, Dopest Album and Hottest Hook

Radio Music Award for Artist of the Year—Hip-Hop Radio

Source Awards for Album of the Year and Single of the Year, Male

2004 Nominated for five Grammy Awards

Nominated for MTV Video Music Award for Best Rap Video

BRIT Award for Best International Breakthrough Artist

2005 American Music Award for Favorite Rap/Hip-Hop Album

Nominated for MTV Video Music Award for Best Male Video and Best Rap Video

2006 Six Grammy Award nominations, including Best Rap Album and Best Rap Song

FURTHER READING

If you enjoyed this biography of 50 Cent, you might also enjoy these other Hip-Hop Superstar biographies from Mitchell Lane Publishers:

Bow Wow *Eminem* *Eve*
Ja Rule *Jay-Z* *Missy Elliott*
Nelly *Queen Latifah* *P. Diddy*
Ice Cube

Works Consulted

Jackson, Curtis James III (50 Cent), with Kris Ex. *From Pieces to Weight: Once Upon a Time in Southside Queens.* New York: Pocket Books, 2005.

"50 Cent Thinks Billboard Flap Will Help Film." Reuters Limited, October 28, 2005.

"50 Cent to Launch 'Street Fiction' Book Line." Associated Press, November 15, 2005.

Armstrong, Dennis. "Live Review: 50 Cent in Ottawa." *Ottawa Sun,* December 22, 2005.

Barnes, Ken. "Radio Heads Up with Carey." *USA Today,* January 3, 2006.

Beggy, Carol, and Mark Shanahan. "'Idol' Scholarship Support; 50 Cent Deals to Avoid Jail." *The Boston Globe,* May 14, 2005, p. C2.

Bejda, Scott. "Interview with 50 Cent." *Murder Dog,* Vol. 12, No. 3, pp. 74–76.

———. "50 Cent: Getting Crucial." *Murder Dog,* Vol. 12, No. 1, pp. 65–70.

Boudicon. "Beauty and the Beast." *YRB,* May/June 2005, Vol. 53, pp. 60–67.

Cane, Clay. "50 Cent: Introducing Curtis Jackson." *Vibe,* January 6, 2006.

Caramanica, Jon. "So Many Diamonds: How Big Can G-Unit Get?" *XXL,* January/February 2006, pp. 88–99.

Derdeyn, Stuart. "The 50 Cent Solution." CanWest News Service, December 18, 2005.

Elwell, Chris. "Fans Get Return From 50 Cent." (London) *Evening Standard,* October 17, 2005.

Eun-jung, Han. "Rapper 50 Cent to Go Live in Seoul." *The Korea Times,* January 31, 2006.

Fine, Larry. "75pc 50 Cent." *The* (Australia) *Sunday Times,* January 9, 2006.

Flamm, Matthew. "50 Cent and MTV Create Book Imprint." *New York Business,* November 14, 2005.

Freeman, John. "'Queens' Chronicles Trigger-happy Gangsta Rap." (St. Louis) *Post-Dispatch,* November 30, 2005.

Gangel, Jamie (TV interviewer). "I know I scare people. That's actually my job." *The Today Show,* November 9, 2005.

Jeckell, Barry A. "50 Cent, Green Day Reap Major Billboard Music Awards." *Billboard,* December 7, 2005.

Jenkins, Sacha, and Chairman Mao. "We're Crazy in a Good Way!" *Blender,* May 2005, pp. 76–82.

Johnson, Gregory. "Never Personal." *King,* October/November 2005, pp. 104–112.

Klostermann, Chuck. "Hard Candy." *Spin,* April 2005, pp. 75–79.

"The Life of a Hunted Man." *Rolling Stone,* April 3, 2003.

Murphy, Keith. "Number One Spot." *XXL,* March 2005, pp. 114–120.

"Police: 50 Cent Movie Sparking Violence Between Rival Gangs." Associated Press, November 30, 2005.

Rayner, Ben. "50 Cent Hosts Policeman's Ball." *Toronto Star,* December 21, 2005.

Romando, Tony. "50 Cent's Gadget Beat-Down." *Sync,* October 1, 2005.

Samuels, Allison. "The Flip Side of 50 Cent." *Newsweek,* February 21, 2005.

Saltzman, Marc. "'50 Cent: Bulletproof' Produces Stale Gameplay." *USA Today,* December 8, 2005.

Stowe, Stacey. "A Wealthy Hartford Suburb Longs, Vainly, for a Rap-Star Neighbor's Company." *The New York Times,* February 17, 2005.

Weiner, Jonah. "Dear Superstar: 50 Cent." *Blender,* April 2005, pp. 66–69.

On the Internet

50 Cent's official website
http://www.50cent.com

INDEX